Hydroponics for Beginners

The Ultimate Hydroponics Crash Course in 30 Minutes or Less!

Copyright © 2015

Table of Contents

Introduction

First and foremost I want to thank you for downloading the book, Hydroponics for Beginners

The Ultimate Hydroponics Crash Course in 30 Minutes or Less!

In this book you will learn how to use hydroponics to grow plants. You will be introduced to all of the types of hydroponics systems and be able to determine which system is best for you. You will learn how to choose which medium you need for your hydroponics system as well as which mediums work best together.

This book is going to teach you how to make two hydroponics systems on your own and how to grow your plants in them and at the end of this book you are going to be given a list of tips that will help ensure your success at using a hydroponics system.

Thanks again for downloading this book, I hope you enjoy it!

Chapter 1

What Is Hydroponics

Hydroponics is a system that is used to grow plants without using the natural method of growing in soil. When you use hydroponics you use other mediums such as water. We will go over the different types of mediums later on in this book but when you are using hydroponics you will use one of these mediums along with a nutrient mixture to grow your plants.

Many people claim that growing plants in a hydroponics system is much healthier than growing them naturally and that the food is more flavorful than if it is grown naturally.

The earliest known publication on growing plants without soil was published in 1627. After this publication the research of growing plants in water became more popular and it was found that plants grew better in water that had not been purified than they did in distilled water. This research of growing plants in water was called water culture.

Growing plants in a nutrient rich solution was later discovered and today this technique is still used but is known as growing plants with no medium. One way you would use this type of system is if you were growing your plants you would have a mister or sprayer come on periodically to spray the roots of the plants with a nutrient rich solution.

Because the word 'hydro' means water, many people think that they have to grow their plants in water but in this book you are going to learn about the many different systems that can be used. You don't have to only use water to grow your plants but you must remember that no matter what you use as a medium your plants will need water.

Many people also believe that growing in hydroponics systems is very complicated but the truth is that it does not have to be. In this book I am going to break these systems down for you so that you will be able to understand just how simple it is to use hydroponics to grow you plants.

This is just how simple hydroponics can be, remember when you were in school and you stuck toothpicks in a potato to suspend the potato over water? Do you remember how you used to watch for the roots to reach to water and finally that green sprout grew out of the top of the potato? This is simple hydroponics. You see, the plant knew that there was water below it and the roots grew so that they could reach the water.

The great thing about hydroponics is that instead of all of the plants energy going into growing a huge root system, the plant only needs a root system large enough to reach the nutrients. Once the roots reach the nutrients, the plant can focus on growing larger and producing larger fruit.

Now you may be wondering what you will need to get started. Of course you will need a system and we will go over how you can build a system of your own later on in this book. You will need nutrients, a medium, a light source, plants and some time.

I will teach you everything you need to know about all of the different things you will need but you do need to understand that hydroponics just like growing plants of any type is going to take some time. It is going to take some work and you are going to have to pay a lot of attention to the small details.

Chapter 2
Hydroponics Systems

Now that you know a little bit about what hydroponics is it is time to learn about the different types of systems. These systems come in many different structures, some may be in large tubs, trays or towers depending on the type you are wanting to use.

There are two basic types of systems, one is a solution system that uses water and a nutrient solution. There is no other medium used, this system is just like when you grow a potato in a cup. The plant roots will grow directly into a nutrient rich solution. The second type of system is known as the aggregate system.

In an aggregate system a medium such as sand, gravel or perlite is used and the plants roots grow into it. Both systems have to have a large amount of water and they both have to have a nutrient rich solution and they have to have oxygen. Different types of plants will do better in different systems and we will learn which ones should be grown in each system as we go through them.

There are several different hydroponic systems that you can use, they are called ebb and flow, static solution, continuous flow, aeroponics, passive sub-irrigation, run to waste, deep water, fogponics, and rotary.

The ebb and flow system is the simplest form of hydroponics and it is recommended that if you have never used a hydroponics system before that you start out with this one. This one works with 2 trays or tubs. One will be placed on top of the other. The top tub will contain a medium such as gravel the bottom tub will contain a nutrient rich solution mixed with water.

The plants are planted into the top tub and using a pump the nutrient solution is periodically pumped into the top tub filled with the medium. You will use a run off of some type so that if the top tub fills up too much while the pump is pumping, the nutrient rich solution will simply drain back into the bottom tub. After the top tub has been filled with the solution it will slowly drain back into the bottom tub and the process will start again.

The pros of an ebb and flow system are that it is easy to build, most of these can be made at home using materials that you already have or can purchase for a low price. This system is also easy to maintain. It does not require a lot of technical knowledge and if you purchase the system it is basically a plant and grow system.

This type of system provides a huge amount of nutrients to the plants since it is always filling up with the nutrient rich solution and provides as much water to the plants as they need. This is especially good for growing plants such as strawberries that need a lot of water.

This system is usually the cheapest type of system to purchase and if you are building it yourself it is also extremely cheap.

The down side of using this type of system is that you have to be very careful that your pump does not go out. If a pump were to go out and the plants were to be without water and nutrients for as few as a couple of hours the plants will die. Another con of this system is that over time with the constant filling and draining of water, salt can build up on the roots of the plants causing them to not be able to absorb the nutrients they need.

You also have to monitor the PH levels very carefully when using an ebb and flow system because since the water is constantly flowing into the top tub and draining back into the hold tank, the PH levels can change drastically. If this is not monitored it can cause your plants to not be able to absorb the nutrients they need thus killing them.

A static solution system is when plants are grown in a container of nutrient rich solution. This system is much like growing a potato in a cup but you can use any container, buckets, tubs or jars. This is usually used for indoor growing but can also be used outdoors. If you are using a container that is clear you will need to cover it to reduce the chances of algae growing. Many people choose to use black plastic to cover their containers. If algae grows, it will take all of the nutrients out of the solution as well as all of the oxygen therefore killing your plants.

The containers that you will use will be called your reservoirs, you can have one plant per reservoir or multiple plants but you must keep in mind that as the plants grow they will need bigger reservoirs.

It is important that your plants have enough oxygen. Since your nutrient rich solution will not be flowing you will need to add oxygen to your water. You can do this by simply using an aquarium pump. Another thing you will have to do is make sure that you are changing out the solution on a regular basis. This can be done on a schedule or when the nutrient levels fall below what is desired. You have to do this because if you allow the plant to suck up all of the nutrients in the water and never replace them than your plants will die. The water has to be changed on a regular basis because there are nutrients in the water that the plant needs. Not doing so will only cause the plant to be nutrient deficient.

A continuous flow system is the next system I want to discuss. In this system the nutrient rich solution continuously flows past the roots of the plants. This system is much easier than using the static system because you are able to check the PH levels as well as the temperature of the water in the large storage tank which the water flows out of. You also don't have to worry about changing multiple containers since there is only one tank of solution for the entire system.

Another variation of this system is to allow a small amount of nutrient rich solution to flow through a shallow area where the roots will form a thick mat. These roots will absorb all of the nutrient rich solution the plants need but the top portion of the roots will be out of the solution allowing them to absorb as much oxygen as they need.

To properly design a system like this you will have to ensure that it is set on a slope, you will have to ensure that the correct slope is being used as well as the correct flow rate. It is important to note that it has been reported that when a channel is longer than 12 meters long plants have a much slower growth rate.

This system is also very cheap to use and it like the ebb and flow system has a grow bed that is separated from the reservoir. Many people will put fish in the reservoir and this is called aquaponics. Aquaponics is much more complicated than hydroponics because you have to ensure that you have the correct amount of fish or your plants will end up over fed and unable to clean the water or they will end up underfed and die. We are not going to go into depth about aquaponics but it is an option if you use a separate tank as a reservoir for your water and one for your grow bed.

The down side of this system is that the plants roots can become water logged. Water can also become stagnant in the system because the flow will move around any blockages that are created by the roots.

Aeroponics is the next type of system I want to talk about. When you are using this system, the roots of the plant will be continually misted with a nutrient rich solution. When you use this system, the plants are suspended in a container of nothing but air, the sprayers will mist the roots providing them with enough nutrients but ensuring that they do not become water logged as well as ensuring that the plants do not drown.

One of the great benefits to this type of system is that unlike many of the other systems, any type of plant can be grown using aeroponics. Since the plants are able to receive 100 percent of the oxygen, carbon dioxide and nutrients that it needs, the rooting time is reduced which allows the plant to grow larger more quickly and produce much larger fruit.

Another great benefit to this type of system is that the plants will not suffer shock if they are transplanted into soil unlike when the other hydroponic systems are used.

Passive sub-irrigation is another system that you can use to grow your plants. This system is used when a porous material is used to transport the water and nutrients to the root of the plant by absorbing it from the reservoir.

This system is great for plants that need a lot of oxygen to their roots and it also is reduces the chances of root rot because just like if the plant were in soil the roots have to work to get the water and nutrients.

A run to waste system is much like an ebb and flow system meaning that the plants are in a tub and the nutrient rich solution is pumped from the reservoir into the growing tub. The difference is that once the nutrients have been depleted from the water instead of just turning it into waste, the water is processed through a filtration system so that it can be used multiple times. This system also waters from the top unlike when you use the ebb and flow system which waters from the bottom of the system.

Perlite and sand are popular mediums that can be used in this type of system and is great to grow plants such as tomatoes, cucumbers and various peppers in.

A deep water system is when the roots of the plant are suspended in water that is nutrient rich and is oxygenated. You will need to put an air pump in the water to ensure that the plant is able to get enough oxygen and does not drown. You also have to be careful when using this type of system to ensure that the roots do not become water logged. This type of system is known for producing much larger plants because of the large amount of oxygen that the plant is able to absorb from the water.

Fogponics is when the nutrients and water are transferred to the plant in the form of vapor, thus the name "fog"ponics. You will use the concept of growing the plant in a container with nothing as a medium but air just like when you use areoponics but the plants will be misted with a vapor using a timer.

As you can see there are many different types of hydroponics systems for you to choose from and you may be wondering exactly how you will choose which system will work best for you. You will need to look at the amount of money you are willing to spend, your specific needs depending on what type of plant you are growing, for example none of the systems that use sprayers work well with organic plants because the organic plant food tends to clog up the sprayers.

You will also want to look at how much experience you have with hydroponics. If you are a beginner I suggest that you start out with a simple ebb and flow system and see if that works out for you. If on the other hand you have been using hydroponics for a while you can use a more complicated system.

Finally you want to look at the amount of time that you have to spend maintaining the system as well as the plants. If you have a lot of time to focus on the system you may choose to go with a manual system where you will be manually feeding and watering the plants on a schedule, if you don't have the amount of time needed for that you will want to go with an automated system but you take the risk of it breaking and your plants dying.

No one can tell you which system you need to choose because it all depends on what you want to put in, but by using the information I have just given you, you will be able to make the right choice for you, your plants, and your lifestyle.

Chapter 3
Mediums

I have mentioned several times so far in this book different types of mediums that you can use in your hydroponics systems. So I want to spend just a little bit of time discussing the different types of mediums that you can use.

If you are using a system where the medium will absorb the nutrient rich water and deliver it to the plants, the best type of medium you can use is cotton or perlite. These will allow the plant to get the oxygen it needs while insuring the plant also has access to the nutrients and water needed to grow. This works much like growing the plant in soil and is the least used type of system.

There are many other mediums that you can use in the different types of systems but before we discuss that further you need to make sure that before you put any medium into your system that you rinse it thoroughly. These mediums are usually covered in dust and although you will never be able to get all of the dust off and for the first few water changes you will notice the dust in the water it is best to get as much off as possible to ensure it does not build up on the roots of the plants.

Rockwool is one of the most popular mediums that hydroponics users put in their systems. It is a sterile medium that is made out of lime or granite that has been heated up and then spun in to small threads often looking much like cotton candy.

Rockwool is porous so it sucks water up very easily. The only issue with this medium is that you have to ensure that it does not become too saturated because if it does it will suffocate your plants or could lead to root rot. You will also have to make sure that the rockwool is PH balanced before you place it in your system and this is done by soaking it in PH balanced water.

Grow rock, also known as hydrocorn is a type of clay that has been fired in a way so that it creates a porous texture. Grow rock is light weight but it is still heavy enough to keep your plants in place. Grow rock has a neutral PH level so you don't have to worry about it affecting the PH levels of your water, it will also absorb the nutrient rich water wicking it up to the roots of your plants. Grow rock is sterile and it can be used multiple times as long as it is cleaned and sterilized between each use. This is another very popular medium and most stores that carry hydroponic supplies will carry grow rock as well.

Coco Fiber and Coco chips are made from the shell of a coconut and used as a medium when growing using a hydroponics system. This was once considered a waste product but today is known as one of the best hydroponic growing mediums available. Although this is a natural material it breaks down very slowly so it does not provide any additional nutrients to whatever is growing in it which is one reason it is so useful in hydroponics. Placing this on the ground when growing plants using the traditional method would not benefit the plants at all but using it as a medium in a hydroponics system works great because it is able to absorb the nutrient rich solution and deliver it to your plants as it is needed. The only difference between coco fiber and coco chips is the size, coco fiber is very fine and has the consistency of potting soil but coco chips are much larger and resemble wood chips.

The chips will allow for air pockets between the chips which allows more oxygen to get to the roots of the plants. When you purchase both the chips and the fiber they will come in a compressed brick. You will soak these bricks and they will expand to about 6 times their original size. These do tend to color the water in your reservoir but this will not harm your plants and if you are concerned about it you can reduce the chances of your water being colored by soaking the medium two to three times changing the water in between each soak.

Perlite is another medium that can be used. Perlite is a natural substance that is composed of minerals, when the perlite is heated it pops like popcorn and becomes very light. This is what you will find in potting soil, it is the small white balls. Perlite is porous, has a neutral PH, works great for wicking but perlite alone is usually not the best choice as a medium. This is because perlite becomes so light once it is popped that it will float. You can find perlite at any nursery as well as many building supplies stores. But when working with it you need to make sure you do not get the dust in your eyes, if you do make sure you wash them out with cold water and always make sure to wash the dust off of your skin after working with perlite because it can cause allergic reactions.

Vermiculite is a material that expands when it is exposed to high heat just like perlite does. When used as a growing medium it is very similar to perlite except that it can hold nutrients for later use. This is another medium that is very light and should not be used on its own because it tends to float. There are different types of vermiculite and each has a specific use so you need to make sure that you are getting the type of vermiculite that is intended for growing plants. The best way to ensure you get this type of vermiculite is for you to purchase it from a nursery.

Grow stones are made out of recycled glass and are very much like grow rocks but unlike grow stones they are unevenly shaped. Although they are made out of recycled glass they are not sharp so you do not have to worry about getting cut. They are light weight as well as porous they allow oxygen to get to the roots of the plant while still ensuring that they are kept moist without allowing them to become water logged. Grow stones are great to use for wicking because they can absorb the nutrient rich solution and wick it up to 4 inches above the water line. You have to be careful when using a medium such as this because if you allow the solution to be wicked all the way to the top of the grow stones you can have problems such as stem rot.

River rocks are a very common as well as easy to find medium that you can use in your hydroponics system. You can purchase these at home improvement stores as well as any pet store that sells fish or aquarium supplies. These ae usually pretty cheap depending on where you purchase them. They are usually round and smooth which is caused from the river water forcing to tumble down the river but you will usually be purchasing river rock that is manufactured but the results will be the same.

River rocks are very heavy so if you are going to use this for a medium if you are going to use very many you want to make sure you will not have to move the container later. Since river rocks are not porous they cannot be used for picking up the nutrient rich solution to the plants roots. They do allow for large spaces between each other so the roots are able to get plenty of oxygen. Since the rocks will not hold moisture you will need to make sure the watering schedules are adjusted so that the roots do not dry out. River rocks are best used in an ebb and flow type of system.

Since the rocks are smooth and water will easily be able to drain off of them, you may want to use another medium with them such as perlite that will absorb some of the nutrient rich solution and ensure that your roots do not dry out. If you are using a wicking system, adding a layer of river rocks at the bottom of your grow tub then covering it with the wicking medium will ensure that the lighter medium does not drain out into your reservoir tub and it will also ensure that the wicking medium does not become to saturated thus causing your roots to rot or your plants to smother.

Pine shavings are a great inexpensive medium that can be used in hydroponic systems. Many of the large commercial growers use pine shavings and it is best used in a drip system. If you do decide to use pine shavings you need to make sure that they were kiln dried and that it does not contain any chemicals. You also need to make sure that you are getting pine shavings and not a bunch of saw dust. If you get a bunch of saw dust, it will become water logged and will drown your plants.

The pine shavings have to be kiln dried because this is how the sap is burned off of the pine, sap will kill your plants if it is not burned off so it is very important that you know how the shavings were dried. You can find pine shavings at a feed store because it is often used for animal bedding but you need to check and make sure there are no chemicals added including odor inhibitors, usually purchasing organic pine shavings ensures there are no chemicals.

Since pine shavings are a natural wood product, they are porous meaning that they will absorb the nutrient rich solution very easily which also means that they can become water logged very easily. This is another medium that can be used with river rocks to ensure your plants do not drown.

Of course there are many other mediums that you can use in your hydroponics system and there is no way that I could ever cover them all but these are the most popular types. If none of these work for you, you may consider rice hulls, polyurethane foam or even sand.

It is extremely important when you are choosing your hydroponics system that you choose the right medium to meet your needs, provides the biggest yields and is easiest for you to maintain. Take your time when choosing your medium and make sure that it will work well with the system you are using.

Chapter 4
How To Create Your Own System

I want to spend a little bit of time discussing how you can create your own hydroponics system. Of course you can purchase these systems but it is very simple to make some of your own.

Many of the items that you will need for this project can be found around your house or they can be purchased much cheaper than if you bought the system from a manufacturer.

You will need to make sure that if you are using a pump of any sort that the cord is long enough so that it does not pose a hazard. You do not want water getting on the outlet that you are using so you need to ensure your cord will be long enough for you to keep your system far away from your outlet. If you are unable to do this the first thing you need to do is call an electrician so that they can install a waterproof outlet.

For this project you will need, 2 buckets the larger of the two buckets needs to be double the size of the smaller bucket or tub. For example if the smallest tub which will be what you are planting in is 40 gallons you will need the large bucket to be 80 gallons.

You will also need a medium and for this project I recommend that you use river rocks as well as perlite or some other porous medium. You will need a pump that will pump the water from one tank to the other, two hoses, fittings for both ends of the hoses an air pump, one that is used in an aquarium is fine for this system, a timer if you want to use it. It is an option to use a timer but it will automate your system so that you don't have to worry about your plants drying out. Another thing that will ensure that your plants do not dry out is adding the perlite to the river rocks as a medium.

The last things you will need is your plants, water and nutrients. I will nutrients a little bit later but this is a mixture that you will use to feed your plants.

The first thing you want to do is drill two holes in the bottom of your smaller tank. These are going to be where you will attach your pump and drain hose. Once these holes are drilled place your pump in the tank. You want to make sure that the top of the pump allows for water to drain back into the reservoir if the grow tank gets too full. Attach your hoses and both of your fittings. Place your air pump in the bottom tank, this is used to ensure that the water has enough oxygen in it and that the nutrient stays mixed in with the water. Place the grown tank on top of the reservoir tank, this will allow gravity to naturally pull the water back down into the reservoir tank. If you will be adding a timer this is the point in which you would want to do that.

Now you want to thoroughly clean your medium. Make sure that you remove as much dust as possible. Many different mediums will change the color of your water if they are not washed properly. This is not usually a problem and it will go away after a few water changes but it is best if you can get as much dust off of the medium as possible.

After you have cleaned the medium, you will want to fill up your grow tank with the medium. You want to make sure that the medium is about 2 inches higher than the drain off of the pump. This will ensure that your plants do not drown and your roots do not rot. Now you want to mix your nutrient solution with the water.

There are many different types of nutrient solutions available and each one will tell you how to mix it and in what proportions. When you are first starting a plant you will want to use about half of the regular amount of nutrients, once the plant begins to grow fruit you will want to increase the nutrients up to the amount suggested on the package.

There are specific things that you need to look for when you are choosing which nutrient solution you should purchase. You need to make sure that the solution you choose includes the following, nitrogen, phosphorus, potassium, calcium, magnesium, and sulfur. Many solutions will contain other minerals but these are the basic nutrients, if a solution does not contain one of these minerals your plants will be deficient and will not grow properly.

Now you are ready to test your system and make sure that it all works. If everything works out than you can add your plants. If there is a problem with the system you will be able to fix it before adding your plants.

This system is an ebb and flow system and if you have never worked with hydroponics before I suggest that you start with a system like this. The reason for this is that if you decide that hydroponics is not something you want to invest your time in, you have not invested very much money. This is a great system for beginners also because if there is a problem with the system it is very easy to fix as well as very cheap.

You can create as many of these systems as you want to plant all of the food you want to grow, just remember that when you have this type of system you want to do an entire solution change at least once every two weeks, of course you will have to do it more if you find that your nutrients are being absorbed before the two weeks is over. This will really depend on the amount of plants you have in each growing tank.

You can make your own water culture system by filling up any type of tank with your nutrient rich solution. Remember that if the tank is see through you will either need to paint it black or cover it to insure that there is not algae growth in the tank because this will disrupt the growth of the plants and the algae will take all of the nutrients and oxygen out of the water.

You will have to be able to see the water level so you can do this by applying a strip of painters tape from the top of the tank to the bottom before painting it so that you can peel this off later allowing you to monitor the water levels.

Next you will need to measure the tank so that you have the exact dimensions, cut a piece of Styrofoam ¼ of an inch smaller than the opening of the tank. The Styrofoam should fit nicely in the tank leaving just enough room so that it can adjust to water level changes.

Now you will need to cut holes for the net pots in the Styrofoam. Place the net pots on the Styrofoam and use a pencil to draw a circle around the pot. Then cut the holes out of the foam. On one end of the foam you will need to cut a small hole for the air hose to run into the reservoir.

You will need to make sure that whatever pump you use is strong enough to provide enough oxygen to your plants. You can do this by going to your hydroponics supply store and telling them the size of your tank as well as the number of plants you will be placing in it. They will be able to tell you which pump will work best for you. Connect your airline to your pump and run the air line through the foam. After the line is run through the foam, you will attach your air stone.

Now you are ready to fill your reservoir with the nutrient solution, place the foam in the tank, fill your net pots with your growing medium and place one plant in each one of your pots. Place each of your net pots in the designated holes and turn on your pump. Now your system is finished.

Of course there are many other systems that you can use and they are all just as easy to make. Of course I cannot include how to make every type of system in this book but I am hoping that by reading this chapter you have learned just how easy hydroponics can be. In the last chapter of this book I am going to give you some tips to help ensure that you are successful at using hydroponics systems.

Chapter 5
Tips for Using Hydroponics

To finish up this book, I want to give you the tips you need to ensure that you are successful at using a hydroponics system.

1. Make sure that you pay attention to the temperature of the solution. You want to make sure that you keep the temperature of the solution is between 65 and 73 degrees. You want to do this because the roots need to be kept at the temperature they would naturally be if they were under ground. If the temperature drops too low it will slow the growing process and if the temperature raises too much it can kill your plants. One way to ensure that the temperature is kept at the appropriate level is to add a thermostat to the reservoir tank as well as a heater and a cooler. If the temperature gets too high you will simply cool the tank and if it gets too low all you have to do is heat the tank until the water is at the correct temperature.

2. If you are growing your plants outside, you need to make sure that they are getting the appropriate sunlight for optimal growing. You will also want to place plants that need the same amount of sunlight in the same growing tanks.

3. If you are growing your plants indoors you need to remember that they will use more water than if you were growing them outside so you need to keep a watch on your water levels.

4. If you are growing your plants indoors you also need to consider lighting. Plants are going to need as much natural light as possible but if natural light is not an option than you need to make sure you are getting the strongest bulbs possible.

5. Many people ask how often they should set their timers for when it comes to watering their plants, this is a difficult question to answer because you need to take a few things into consideration. You need to think about the type of medium you are using, for example if you are using river rocks with no other medium the solution is going to drain off of the roots very quickly so you want to make sure the grow tank is filled quickly after it empties. On the other hand if you are using a porous medium that absorbs the solution, you will want to set the timer

for a longer period of time so that your plants do not suffer from root rot or become water logged.

6. Make sure that you do not damage the root system when you are transplanting into a hydroponics system. Any damage to the roots will result in the plant dying because it will not be able to absorb the nutrients needed. If you are transplanting from soil you don't have to worry about getting all of the soil off of the roots, the nutrient solution will wash the soil off and you will remove it from your reservoir tank with your first change. Trying to remove all of the soil from the roots will just result in damage and that needs to be avoided at all cost. You can also take the plant and place the roots in a bucket of warm water simply allowing the water to remove the soil from the roots.

7. Take some time to learn about plants and growing. If you have never grown plants before you will need to take some to learn about how plants grow and what their needs are. You should also take some time to learn about the signs of disease, what the leaves of each plant should look like, why plant leaves turn yellow and so on. You need to also take time to focus on each specific plant that you are growing. Learn the needs of each plant such as the specific lighting they need and the different types of nutrients they need.

8. Even though the plants are getting plenty of water from their roots, you need to make sure that you are spraying the leaves on a regular basis. You don't have to spray them with a nutrient rich solution simple water will do but plants naturally absorb water through their leaves so you need to allow them to go through this process.

9. One mistake many people make is that they give their plants carbon dioxide. Plants produce this naturally and giving them extra will only harm the plant. If the plant is growing outside you never have to worry about this and simply opening a window if they are grown inside will give them what they need to produce the amount of carbon dioxide that they need.

10. Always watch for bugs of all types. This is especially important if you are growing your plants outside because bugs will be able to get to them more easily but it is also important if

you are growing your plants inside. You should turn over the leaves of the plants to make sure there are not bugs under the leaves or any eggs. You need to check for holes in the leaves or any area where a bug has been eating the leaves of the plants.

11. If you live in an area where the tap water contains a lot of chemicals you will need to find a source of pure clean water to use for your system. Well water works fine as well as rain water if you are not in an extremely polluted area. If there is a lot of pollution in the area and you use tap water or rain water for your system the plants will become poisoned. Even if you use a water softener and filter for you water it will contain minerals that will kill your plants.

12. Make sure that you clean your tanks thoroughly between different plants. You may find that once the harvest season is over you want to grow a different plant in your grow tub or you may decide that you want to grow the same type of plant. It is important to make sure you clean and sterilize your tanks in between these plants because you do not want any diseases to be spread, this also ensures that algae does not grow in your tanks. While you are doing this you will want to clean and sterilize your medium if it is one that can be reused.

Conclusion

Thank you again for downloading this book!

I hope this book was able to help you to understand how hydroponics works and how you can put it to use.

The next step upon successful completion of this book is to choose a system, medium and plants, then get started using hydroponics to grow your plants.

Finally, if you enjoyed this book, please take the time to share your thoughts and post a review on Amazon. It'd be greatly appreciated!

Thank you and good luck!

39048301R00018

Made in the USA
Middletown, DE
08 January 2017